# CONGRATULATIONS
## You Just Got Hired

Don't Screw It Up

Robert L Deitz

ISBN: 1481944290
ISBN-13: 9781481944298
Library of Congress Control Number: 2013900675
CreateSpace, North Charleston, South Carolina

# Reviews for Congratulations – You Just Got Hired: Don't Screw It Up

## KIRKUS BOOK REVIEW

A thorough compendium of straightforward, sensible advice for newbies finding their way around their first office jobs.

Deitz graduated with honors from Harvard Law School in 1975 and rose to some of the highest levels in law and government, including service as general counsel of the National Security Agency. So when this heavy hitter tells you to beware of casual dress on the job, you do it. It's difficult to argue with any of the 80 or so items of workaday advice Deitz offers in this slim, well-written guidebook, which covers the essentials of successful on-the-job behavior, dress, etiquette and online activities. ... It's the rare college graduate, new to an office job, who won't benefit from Deitz's writing counsel....

A fine book for a newly hired college graduate who wants to succeed.

## Clarion Review

Five Stars (out of Five)

"The purpose of this book is to provide practical job advice," writes first-time author Robert L. Deitz in his introduction to Congratulations – You Just Got Hired: Don't Screw it Up. He fulfills his goal with humor and brevity. As to his guidance, he has the experience to back it up.

Basing the contents on a lecture he developed for George Mason University's School of Public Policy, Deitz—at the urging of colleagues and friends—has now compiled his thoughts into a well-written and tautly edited guide, one that should be required reading not only for those entering a career for the first time but for everyone in today's work arena.

The advice is driven by twenty-first-century needs and is clearly stated, with personal foibles inserted very sparingly—just enough to make the reader want to know more. …

"The most liberating words in the English language are 'I don't know,'" states Deitz. There seems to be an element of shame in admitting that one does not have an answer, and Deitz breaks through this with clarity and crisp advice. He also touches upon such topics as work habits, avoiding gossip, dealing with the media, and handling confidential information.

Congratulations –You Just Got Hired is the perfect gift for college seniors and anyone else looking for a job in today's volatile job market. It would also be good to have it on hand in any office. Deitz's advice is spot-on, relevant, and a pleasure to read.

# Contents

# Introduction

The purpose of this book is to prevent you from screwing up your first professional job. As a recent college or professional school graduate, you likely have all the intellectual tools necessary to thrive in the professional world. But academic training is only part of the preparation you need to succeed. Unless you know how to comport yourself in the office, there are numerous traps that can ensnare you and short-circuit your career.

This book arose from a two-hour discussion I facilitated at George Mason University's School of Public Policy, during my appointment to the faculty as a CIA officer-in-residence. In one of my classes, some students had asked questions about how professionals conduct themselves at the CIA including questions about appropriate dress and inter-office relations.

Initially these questions struck me as naïve. Later it dawned on me that while graduate students are prepared academically to enter the professions, they may not be practically ready for work life in an office of a large, complex organization. I spoke to a colleague who suggested that I offer an informal discussion for interested students about "life" as a professional.

This guide comes from that discussion and from some materials I created for the purpose. I have lived and worked in the Washington area for more than 35 years. Like many lawyers here, I have held a number of jobs in both the private sector and the government. Also like many others, I have observed promising careers go up in smoke for behaviors having nothing to do with the intellectual challenges of the workplace. I am not speaking here of evil-doers, of criminals, or of psychopaths. Rather, I am referring to well-meaning newbies whose conduct was or was perceived as inconsistent with professional behavior.

It is simply not true that those professionals with the "best," the flashiest, resumes, meaning those who have attended the most prestigious colleges and graduate schools, have earned the highest grades, have held the niftiest internships inevitably rise to the top of their professions. There are many other qualities, few of which are taught in school, that lead to success in the workplace. How you dress, how you behave, how you address bosses and higher ups, how you use email and the internet are all potential traps. This is true even if "everyone does it." The purpose of this book is to provide practical job advice.

None of what follows is complicated; none of this is rocket science. For experienced job holders, little of this will be new. But for those beginning their careers, the suggestions may prove useful, by helping to guide and shape work habits and attitudes. These suggestions should not be taken more seriously than they warrant. For the most part, they should not be viewed as iron laws, but rather as considerations. A friend compares these suggestions to military doctrine, which is a body of thought that has proved useful because it is based on experience, but is not directive.

While my original audience was graduate students in public policy – students presumptively headed for careers in federal, state, and local government or non-governmental organizations – these suggestions apply equally to new college graduates, attorneys, MBAs, accountants and any one else starting a professional job. And while I have been headquartered in Washington, these suggestions are equally relevant to professional life in any office environment in any city. In a fundamental sense, all offices are alike: they are composed of bosses and workers engaged in some common enterprise. While office work requires professional training, success depends equally on knowing how to negotiate office routines.

This book is based on my personal experiences and observations. I started out in entry level jobs at law firms and in the government. Overtime I became more senior. In the process, I learned, sometimes through painful experience, how to avoid the blunders that can undermine one's career and how to negotiate successfully the office environment.

I graduated from Middlebury College (B.A., *cum laude*, Phi Beta Kappa, 1968); The Woodrow Wilson School, Princeton University (M.P.A. 1972); and Harvard Law School (*magna cum laude*, member of the *Harvard Law Review*, 1975). I clerked for Supreme Court Justices Douglas, Stewart, and White in 1975-76. I was a special assistant to the Secretary of the then-Department of Health, Education & Welfare and to the Deputy Secretary of State, both during the Carter Administration. I was a lawyer in private practice for over 20 years and was a litigating partner in two large law firms.

In 1998 I became the general counsel of the National Security Agency. Later I became the acting deputy general counsel for intelligence at the Department of Defense and acting general counsel for the National Geospatial Intelligence Agency. In 2006 I became the senior councilor to the Director of the CIA. I retired from the CIA in 2012 and am now a professor of public policy at George Mason University's School of Public Policy.

In these various private and public sector jobs, I have seen lots of office behavior. I know what conduct will advance careers, what conduct will undermine them. Following these suggestions and guidelines will not, of course, guarantee you success in the workplace. The quality of your work will certainly matter as you move up the career ladder. But following these suggestions and guidelines will help assure that your career is not derailed by your conduct and behavior. Good luck!

CHAPTER 1

# Work Habits

A lot goes on in an office. A lot is irrelevant. Don't let office "noise" interfere with your work.

1. <u>Dealing with the boss.</u> In any office, you will inevitably have a boss. Some bosses are jerks; some are great men and women. If your boss is a jerk, there is little you can do about it, except to learn how to deal with him or her. The best way you can impress is by making your boss's work day easier; to be useful to him or her; to take care of problems. Making problems, even trivial ones, disappear is one of the most important skills known to mankind. Doing so without leaving footprints is even more sublime.

It often pays not to look for credit directly. Doing so could embarrass the boss or make it seem that you are someone who only takes care of things to get praise. You want to be recognized as someone who is indispensable. Unless the problem requires discussion or approval, it is much better to deal with problems quietly. Your boss will notice that his/her life is easier and will eventually understand that you had something to do with that. But do not make decisions that are beyond your competence. Be sure to observe the hierarchies. See paragraph 22, below.

2. <u>Study your boss carefully.</u> Successful people do. (S)He will have a unique vocabulary, speaking style, and sense of humor. After joining a federal agency, I noted how in meetings seniors would use much of the agency director's vocabulary, metaphors, and expressions. When that director was replaced, people began picking up the new director's verbal idiosyncrasies. If your boss is a micromanager, become used to getting down in the weeds over word choices. If your boss is the quiet type, subdued, don't shout and wave your arms in meetings. If (s)he is voluble and wildly gestures, feel free to mimic. When you draft a document for the

1

boss's signature, be sensitive to the way (s)he writes. If your boss hates split infinitives or jargon words or metaphors, avoid them in your drafts.

3. <u>Observe.</u> You will learn many things in any new job. Much of what you are learning will be the business of the office, how to fulfill the assignments you are given. While the business of the office is crucial, of course, it is wise to learn from colleagues and bosses how to comport yourself, how generally to behave. Watch how your boss conducts meetings. Observe how (s)he interacts with her/his boss. Watch how your colleagues behave. Watch the reactions of colleagues and bosses as they observe the behavior of others. From these observations, you will learn a great deal. From these "lessons" you will see behavior that you should emulate; you will also see behavior that you should avoid.

4. <u>Assignments.</u> Accept all assignments that are given to you. As a professional, salaried employee, you should never tell a boss that "that's not my job." As a professional you should never act as if you are working in a job with union-shop rules. If you are first in and last out, your boss will notice. If you are swamped, work longer hours even if you are not eligible for overtime pay. Of course there are subtle ways of letting a boss know that you have been given more assignments than you could possibly complete. One way to do this is by asking your boss to help you prioritize your assignments. Another way is by asking, "Does this assignment have a greater or lower priority than the one you gave me yesterday"?

5. <u>Treat support staff with respect.</u> Secretaries, now often called special assistants in the government and elsewhere, are, alas, increasingly rare in the workplace. If you have a secretary or if there are secretaries or assistants attached to your office, treat them with respect and deference. You may have more formal education, but you decidedly will have less experience. Secretaries and assistants have the confidence of the boss. They know everything about the office. Most important, they are the boss's gatekeeper. If you want an appointment with the boss, if you want to understand his/her preferences and the way the office works, the secretary can be your

sure guide. If you need office supplies or want your computer fixed, the secretary can make that happen.

Treat secretaries or assistants badly, with arrogance and condescension, and they will make your life miserable. In many organizations secretaries have close ties to secretaries in other offices. Treat one of them badly, they will all know it. Moreover, if your boss sees you mistreat his/her secretary, he/she will not be pleased. You will see that most seniors in offices treat secretaries, their own and those of others, well. They do so for a reason: a good secretary is often the key to a smoothly functioning office.

6. <u>Work until the job is done; don't watch the clock.</u> Professional jobs are not like summer jobs at McDonald's, the country club, or Ben & Jerry's. Show up on time, even early, and don't watch the clock so you can leave "on time." Work until the job is done. Overtime pay, if you are entitled to it, will take care of itself. Promotions will arrive in due course. Have the attitude that your job is not an entitlement and that the work comes first. Your boss will notice and approve.

7. <u>Don't get too cozy.</u> Resist the urge – often driven by nerves and anxiety – to reveal too much about yourself to establish rapport with your new coworkers. Even innocent exchanges about your personal life can have unintended consequences. Your early office BFF may turn out to be a complete jerk to whom you earlier bared your soul. Or if, for example, you have explained how you are a new mother or father, or have an aging parent to tend, or need to attend regular religious retreats, a supervisor may eliminate you as a candidate for promotion if (s)he thinks you have too many home or other, non-work commitments. In short, never give coworkers reasons to question your commitment to the job. Of course, you will get to know people better over time and form professional friendships through working together.

8. <u>Beware of eager new office friends.</u> Often when you first join an office, there is someone eager to befriend you. Insecure in a new setting, one is tempted to reciprocate. But beware of that person. (S)He may be the office pariah trying to snare an

unwitting ally.  Similarly, try to avoid becoming someone's best friend, that is, someone with whom you always eat lunch, work out, or are always seen.  Treat everyone the same:  pleasantly, politely, and professionally.  Do not inadvertently find yourself in some sort of office conspiracy or cabal.

9.  Avoid office gossip.  At least until you understand the office dynamics do not join in snarky office exchanges.  When your boss sees you with your new best office friend whispering in the office cafeteria, (s)he may take offense.

10.  Try to keep your work life and your home life separate.  When you are bade a good morning, understand this for what it is: a mundane, polite, and meaningless utterance.  Do not take this as an invitation to launch into a rant about how your boy/girl friend is mistreating you; how your diet isn't working; or why the Giants ought to change quarterbacks.  Most people aren't going to care and may start to avoid you just to escape the trivial pursuit and the lake of me that comprise your life.  When you have learned the lay of the office land and begun to develop friends, certain personal discussions may arise in a natural way.  But bosses and co-workers soon learn who is wandering around the office idly shooting the breeze.  You are being paid to work, not to chat the day away.

11.  Don't whine.  Do not become the office complainer, whining about how "they" are not treating you right, giving you too much work, not appreciating your talents, etc.  If you really don't like or appreciate your job, quit.  But until you quit do not become a drag on office morale.

12.  Focus on work, not the personal stuff.  Avoid becoming the office social butterfly, on the one hand, or social worker, on the other.  You know the types:  they know everyone's birthday and anniversary.  They take collections for birthday and promotion cakes and sympathy cards.  They commiserate over every bad thing that life brings to a co-worker.  They are fonts of dating and child-rearing advice.  Save all that for your friends outside work.  Despite all the current feel good clap-trap about offices being "families," they decidedly are not.  They are places where people work.  It is

unprofessional to focus on the personal at the office. Of course you may sign cards and show up at events others organize.

13. <u>Don't focus on your rights.</u> You will have "rights" in most government, NGO (non-governmental organizations), or private-sector jobs. DO NOT EXERCISE THEM. This is, of course, an overstatement. But everyone in an office quickly becomes aware of the employee who "works to the rule," that is, does only what is required, makes sure (s)he gets the full, allotted lunch time, never misses an opportunity to go to the gym, leaves on the dot of whatever time the work day is supposed to end. At one federal agency where I once worked, some employees actually set alarm clocks to ring ten minutes before day's end. The ten minutes were intended to let them clean up their desks, grab their coats, and be prepared to leap up at the appointed hour, when the stampede to the elevator was truly astonishing. At another agency, some professionals clocked in at the assigned time, but then headed off to the gym for workouts. They included their workout time on their time cards.

Focus on your performance and work product. Avoid wasting energy on identifying real or (more often) imagined inequities. Whatever job you take should be the beginning of a career, not just the beginning of a paycheck.

14. <u>Do not exercise your rights, part II.</u> Some employees go through their careers with chips on their shoulders. If someone looks cross-eyed at them, they will file a complaint with the inspector general or ombudsman (in organizations that have them) or to senior management (in the private sector), claiming that their boss is creating a hostile work environment by harassing them, discriminating against them, being mean to them, etc. Some employees in the public sector file EEO claims virtually every year, not because they believe that they have been discriminated against, but because they view such claims as an integral part – almost a legitimate negotiating tool – of the promotion process. Their reasoning: by filing a claim today their boss next year may want to avoid the hassle and promote them regardless of merit.

People who file routine EEO claims, often called "frequent filers," sabotage their careers. Even though the process is supposed to be confidential, it never is. Soon everyone knows who these malcontents are and will avoid working with them, promoting them, etc. While they may win a battle or two, they will lose the war, meaning a good, fulfilling career. As a friend puts it, don't stumble over quarters to pick up nickels.

15. <u>Act prudently if your boss is acting discriminatorily.</u> Of course, if your boss really is hitting on you or making crude racial, ethnic, or sexual jokes, do something. But act temperately. Start by asking yourself whether what you are reacting to is really sex, age, gender, race, religious discrimination. Ask yourself whether you are being hypersensitive. Don't confuse unlawful discrimination with boorish behavior. Some bosses, men and women, can be incredibly crude, routinely dropping the "F" bomb. Talk calmly with your immediate boss or a trusted colleague. Have your facts in order. Hard evidence is crucial: emails, voice mails, behavior that others have witnessed. If it comes down to your word against that of the person you are accusing, (s)he has an advantage: (s)he is known in the organization and has a track record. You are not and do not. Bear in mind that even if your claim is absolutely valid, the fact that you filed such a claim will trail you, fairly or unfairly, for the rest of your career.

16. <u>Be a team player, but take ownership of your assignments.</u> Be generous in sharing credit and accepting blame. Even if you generated the great idea, have done most of the work on a project, drafted most of a memo or brief, your colleagues will appreciate your generosity when you state that "we" did it. By contrast, do not shy away from accepting responsibility for hose ups. Bosses appreciate someone who says "I screwed up." They soon learn who blames everyone else, including the dog, for their errors.

17. <u>Do not burn bridges.</u> Do not alienate anyone inside or outside your immediate office even if the other person is wrong and obnoxious. If you change offices or if your boss is transferred, don't make your happiness and glee obvious. Your adversary to-

day may be your boss next month. Although cities have lots of people, it is astonishing how small the various professional communities really are. The odds are high that your paths will cross down the road.

18. <u>Admit when you don't know the answer.</u> The most liberating words in the English language are "I don't know." Use them. Your boss will inevitably ask you questions whose answers you are not going to know. Admit it! Just say I don't know and immediately add that you will find out the answer to the question. Then be sure to follow up. Don't assume the boss will forget that (s)he ever asked you about the issue. Do not make up an answer. Many bosses have a really good ear for b.s. If you make up an answer that turns out to be wrong, your reputation is marred.

One way of helping to avoid the problem is to ponder in advance what you would want to know about an issue if you were your boss. Ask yourself the standard newspaper questions: who, what, when, where, why, plus how. Then find out the answer to these questions before the meeting. Be as informed about the issue as you can be. It will give you a sense of confidence and will allow you to get more out of the discussion. Over time this will also build your general expertise in the area you are working in. Being informed will make you a better analytical thinker.

19. <u>Ask questions.</u> Don't be afraid to ask questions of your boss about an assignment because you think questions will make you look stupid or perhaps suggest that your boss can't communicate. An assignment may contain a nuance that you do not fully understand and that may be the key to the entire project. There are few things more frustrating than to spend days on an assignment only to be told that you addressed the wrong question.

20. <u>Don't show up the boss.</u> Never embarrass your boss or show up her or him. Your goal is to help, not to show that you are smarter or better educated. Don't speak at meetings unless asked until you understand the relationship you have with your boss. I am always amused while watching NCIS or Special Victims Unit to see interrogations conducted by two or three people. On TV,

of course, this is to spread the lines among the cast. In real life, if I were interrupted by a junior colleague during questioning, I would be tempted to fire him or her.

In a meeting, your boss may deliberately hold back some information not because (s)he forgot it, but for tactical reasons. S/He may have a careful plan to ask questions in a certain order or to lead the discussion in a certain way. If there is something that your boss has screwed up, speak to him or her behind closed doors. At meetings, if (s)he misspeaks or seems to forget to mention an important point, write a note and surreptitiously slide it in front of him or her.

21. <u>Sharing critical comments.</u> If your boss asks you and others by email for comments on something and if your comments are critical, use the reply button, not the reply all button. See chapter 4, paragraphs. 10, 11, 12, below.

22. <u>Observe the hierarchy.</u> Do not send things to your boss's boss without first consulting your boss and obtaining his/her approval. If you send something to the higher ups without authorization, it could get both you and your boss in trouble. The hierarchy is there for a reason. First, the top dog or client does not want unvetted work product from a newbie or junior. (S)He wants it reviewed and approved by the person in the middle, your boss. Second, your boss does not want to be cut out of the loop. (S)He is responsible and therefore wants to control the communications. Going around the boss is a sure way to make an enemy, probably for life.

23. <u>Quick drafts: Hah!</u> Your boss will ask you for "quick drafts" of things such as letters, memos, position papers, briefs, comments on legislation. Even if (s)he uses the term "draft," do not take that word seriously. However the assignment is phrased, you are being asked to prepare a complete document, with proper headings and sub-headings, proper format, and fully developed arguments all wrapped in stylish prose that is spell checked and grammatically unassailable. (By the way, never rely exclusively on your computer's spell check. It will not catch misused homonyms or other

errors that happen to be real words. A friend once developed a position paper about public education for her boss's testimony. In the car on the way to the legislative hearing, she was prepping her boss by highlighting the important points in the document only to find the phrase "pubic higher education." The spell check had not caught the error, of course. All hundred copies of the paper had to be tossed; she was humiliated.)

24. <u>Use proper language.</u> Although memos and other writings can and should be idiomatic, avoid vulgarisms, texting abbreviations, and street language. (I recently received a paper from a student who referred to a policy maker as "pissed off." This was not an ironic comment.) In general, do not use any slang words or sayings found in the Urban Dictionary.

25. <u>Learn the bureaucratic idiom.</u> It is very likely that your early writings will be heavily edited and rewritten. When this happens, do not sulk or feel insulted. Learn from the experience. Law firms, lobbying organizations, companies, and government bureaucracies have different ways of articulating issues, which you need to learn. You need to learn their language and be able to use it as though it were your mother tongue. And it is just possible that you are not as gifted a writer as your high school English teacher or your mother told you.

26. <u>Accept edits with good humor.</u> Do not fall in love with your own words, style, and arguments: what a friend calls drinking your own bathwater. Even if you do not like other people's comments and think that your original draft is better, incorporate the changes. If there is a substantive problem, ask the person who made the comment to explain it to you, saying something like "I just want to be sure that I understand your comment correctly." You obviously want to avoid including textual changes that are wrong. If you ask about it, the person who made the comment will perhaps realize that it was not apt.

27. <u>Brief low.</u> All of us are tempted to wring from a set of facts every rosy picture, every favorable conclusion we can. This is particularly alluring in the office context when the boss is

asking about a complicated project or complex problem involving a number of different players and moving parts. Exaggerating one's progress or the status of a project is sometimes called in the defense/intelligence community "briefing high," which means providing to the boss the answer that (s)he wants and that you hope, fingers crossed, is true. Avoid that temptation. Brief low. Shoot straight with the boss; don't minimize problems. As awkward as meetings can be when the boss is not hearing what (s)he hopes to hear, it is far worse when you must later return to tell him or her that your (and now his/her) optimism was unwarranted.

28. <u>Bosses hate surprises!</u> Never surprise them, unless with some incredibly good news. The project that just blew up in your face; that angry complaint from Capitol Hill; that call from an outraged client; that embarrassing inquiry from the news media; that "reply all" email that you sent when you meant to push the "reply" button: the only thing worse than having to tell your boss about screw ups is having the boss learn about them on his/her own. Most bosses forgive acknowledged mistakes since they themselves have made them. By not giving him/her a heads up, however, you show that not only are you fallible, but you are also a coward. Bosses want with them in the trenches people whom they can trust. That doesn't mean perfect people; it means people with backbones. When you screw up, fess up.

29. <u>Bosses hate surprises, part II.</u> Sooner or later you will be asked to prep your boss for an important meeting inside or outside your organization, for a hearing on Capitol Hill, for a press conference, for a pitch to the client. Take this assignment seriously. Preparations for these events often entail a practice session of questions and answers, called moot courts by lawyers, murder boards at DOD and in the intel community. Do not hold back; do not throw softballs; ask the really hard questions. (Think of this as an acceptable opportunity to get back at your boss for some transgression.) If your boss is asked a question for which (s)he has no answer during an important meeting, you have let him or her down. Once at a hearing on Capitol Hill, my boss was asked

a question that I should have, but had not, anticipated. He very slowly turned in his chair and glared at me. I was mortified.

30. <u>Don't talk in meetings.</u> Of course that injunction is over-stated. As a newbie, however, it is unlikely that anyone will care about your opinion; you won't know enough to have an intelligent one. Moreover, long experience tells me that much of what is said in meetings, whether in government or the private sector, is blather. Think before you say something stupid. Too many people somehow subscribe to the notion that "I talk, therefore I am." If you want to make a point, but that point has been fairly addressed by a previous speaker, resist the urge to repeat it in a slightly different variation. Don't think that if you say nothing in a meeting that you will be thought stupid. The odds are well in the other direction. Everyone soon learns who it is that just has to say something no matter how inane and insignificant. Before you speak, ask yourself three questions:

1) What precisely is it that I want to say?
2) Is my point sufficiently different from what others are saying that it needs to be made?
3) Does the point I want to make conflict with something my boss just said?

When you do speak, do so crisply. It is astonishing how people will make a trivial point, then repeat it two or three times in variations as if their audience were idiots. Your goal is to develop a reputation that when you do speak, you will have something important to say. You do not want to be one of those people – and every organization has them – who, when they begin to speak, cause everyone else in the meeting to roll their eyes.

31. <u>Give your great idea to the boss.</u> If you have a really brilliant idea, tell your boss before the meeting. Let him or her suggest it and take credit for it. Your job is to make your boss look good, not to outshine him or her. This will in turn make him/her think highly of you, and people will know it. You will build your

reputation without showing up your boss. You also avoid embarrassing yourself if the brilliant idea turns out to be nonsense. If you first bring it up with the boss, (s)he can decide if it is worth pursuing.

32. <u>Look prepared.</u> When your boss or anyone else calls you to a meeting, take paper and pen with you, or where allowed, a laptop or iPad. Your attendance without these implements bespeaks your view that the meeting is of little importance. Yes, you may have been a waiter at a New York City steak house and can remember without notes all the orders, including how everyone wants his/her steak cooked, for a table of eight. Nevertheless, take pen and paper to meetings even if you do nothing with them but doodle.

33. <u>Always post.</u> As Woody Allen said, ninety percent of life is showing up. When a project is due or a hearing is to be held or a meeting convened, show up no matter how you feel. Always post. (I once for fun did a chart for my office showing what days of the week had the most claimed sick leave. As you might expect, Fridays and Mondays had the most sick days, Tuesdays and Thursdays far fewer, and Wednesdays the fewest. What a surprise, since you would think that illnesses would be randomly distributed across all days of the week!) Do not think of sick days as mini-vacation opportunities.

34. <u>Tell the truth.</u> If you work in the government, it is possible that you may be asked to speak with an inspector general (IG) or, if you are in the private sector, to speak with senior managers or lawyers about ethical matters. If this happens, cooperate and, for sure, tell the truth. It is a Washington truism that the initial bad act is not what gets people into trouble. Rather, it is the subsequent lies and attempts to cover up the misdeed that sink careers.

I have repeatedly seen cases where an IG was investigating the breach of an agency rule. If the target of the investigation had fessed up, apologized, and promised to be a good boy/girl from then on, the case would have ended. But the person would deny the claim and cook up some lame excuse. When the IG put the lie to that untruth, the consequences were severe, sometimes involving termination or some other career killing penalty. Bosses enjoy magnanimously forgiving minor ethical misdemeanors. Lying to the IG or to seniors in firms and companies is not a minor ethical misdemeanor!

35. <u>Beware of the press.</u> Most experienced reporters are skilled at prizing information from unsuspecting sources. Young office workers are especially good targets. It is flattering, after all, to be called by a reporter. It is something to brag about to one's friends. However, never talk to the press unless you have explicit permission from your boss, which you probably will never receive. The press is why government agencies and many private organizations have experienced press officers.

36. <u>Don't share confidential information.</u> Early in your professional career, perhaps on your very first day, you will learn confidential information: information about clients and their finances and perhaps their legal difficulties; about proposed government legislation or programs or regulations; about strategic advertising plans. This information, no matter how juicy, is not imparted to you so as to make you a more amusing dinner guest. It is not to be blabbed when you meet up with your friends at happy hour. Sharing confidential information not only may violate various professional codes of conduct; it also may violate the law. Worst, it shows that you have no ethical compass and that you do not deserve to be a professional because you cannot be trusted. Revealing confidential information can lead to insider trading, IP theft, the loss of a political campaign or a trial. It will discredit your character and may end your career.

37. <u>Be up on the news.</u> Most offices expect their professional employees to be knowledgeable about current events. And this means more than knowing the latest sports standings or what starlet just got a nose ring. For those of us of a certain age, this means reading or at least scanning each day *The N.Y. Times, The Washington Post, The Wall Street Journal,* or some other legitimate broad sheet. News weeklies, particularly publications like *The Economist,*

are useful. If your preferred medium is the net, these journals can be read on line. The point here is simply that professionals need to be on top of the news, and as you move up the ladder in your career what is in the news may have a serious impact on your work day.

38. <u>Don't drink and drive.</u> Most bosses make a sharp distinction between what you do at work and what you do on your own time. Increasingly, however, drunk driving is becoming an exception. In some positions and offices, if you are arrested for DWI, you will be fired. And even if you are not dismissed, a DWI will harm your career. There is simply no reason to drink and drive. If you live in the city, walk or take public transportation to and from bars and restaurants. If public transportation is out, take a cab. They aren't that expensive. Think of cabs as a cheap form of work insurance.

39. <u>Mentoring.</u> Do try to seek out a positive mentoring relationship. Find someone you respect and seek his/her counsel often. Go to lunch together, for example. (S)He may well be flattered. In some work places it is hard to get ahead without someone more senior clearing a path for you by, for example, praising your diligence and hard work. People who benefit from mentors are more likely to return the favor when they are in a position to do so. If mentoring works the way it is supposed to, everyone wins.

CHAPTER 2

# Dress

Dress appropriately. The office hallway is not the fashion show runway.

1. <u>Dress like a professional.</u> As the old saw has it, clothes make the man or woman. Your clothing is the first thing people notice. Of course, you may dress with style, with panache. But provocative clothes that draw attention to yourself because they are ultra-sexy or revealing or outré will not help you. When in doubt, go for the more restrained look. The office hallway is not the runway.

2. <u>What not to wear.</u> Some work environments are increasingly casual. Most government offices tend to be rather conservative. Use your boss's dress code as a guide. Some items should never be worn (unless you are going undercover for some spook agency): tee shirts, tank tops (aka wife-beater shirts), short shorts, halter tops, tennis shoes, sweat pants, flip-flops, etc. In most government offices, the senior employees dress more formally. The top floors of State, Defense, CIA, for example, are peopled with men in suits and ties and women in comparable business attire. Your goal is to move up, literally, in these agencies. Shoes should be shined, shirts ironed, suits dry-cleaned and pressed. Men always look better in long-sleeved business shirts rather than short-sleeved. Dark business suits and other outfits, particularly if your clothing budget is limited, are preferable to light colors. Get your hair cut regularly and don't wear ill-fitting or ratty clothes, even if they are your favorites. If your boss and colleagues do not routinely wear suits, business shirts, and ties, keep a set in the office for emergency use. You never know when your division or agency head or, in the private sector, a client may call you for a meeting.

3. <u>Beware of "casual day" dress.</u> Even if your office wear is deemed "casual" on certain days, interpret "casual" narrowly. For

men, a sport jacket with slacks is preferable to blue jeans and a polo shirt. For women, the equivalent: look well put together, but don't dress for a date. Flip-flops, shorts, tank tops, and the like should never be worn on casual days. Use your boss's dress as a model.

4. <u>Grooming.</u> This should not need saying, but many years in various offices and bureaucracies tell me that it is worth emphasizing. Practice good hygiene. Shower and change clothes every day. Brush your teeth. See a dentist regularly. Your colleagues will appreciate it. Avoid extreme or extremely complicated hair styles. Forswear elaborate nail designs. Facial hair should be moderate. If you sport tats, cover them up. Reconsider easily visible, extreme facial and body piercings. No boss will ever take you to a meeting if your face/tongue/lips/eyebrows look as though they have been riveted, that is, even assuming that you are hired in the first place.

A friend once hired an administrative assistant who had a masters degree in English. For the interview he was dressed nicely and sported one ear piercing. By the end of the second month, his earrings numbered four or five, the trousers, chinos, had ripped hems because they were now too long, and he walked on them with sandals without socks. At the holiday party for 13,000 employees, he looked like a fool.

5. <u>Avoid the persistent aromas.</u> Lose the perfumes, the after shaves, the hair sprays and gels. Get rid of the scented oils and candles on your desk. Many people are allergic to these aromas; over time, their smells can overpower an office.

6. <u>Practice taste and restraint.</u> In sum, if your clothes and style announce you at all, they should bespeak taste and restraint.

# CHAPTER 3

# Etiquette

The workplace is not the frat house or sorority. Adopt Granny's etiquette standards.

1. <u>Manners and language.</u> Two of the most important qualities that interviewers and bosses notice are table manners and language. Don't let them trip you up. When you eat like Homer Simpson – hunched over your plate, elbows on the table, mouth stuffed with food, spearing your food as though it were about to flee – your boss will notice. If you speak ungrammatically or foully, (s)he will notice. About manners generally, if your grandmother would be upset by something, don't do it. (A friend tells of a meeting where one attendee emitted a loud, earth swallowing yawn without covering her mouth.)

2. <u>Jokes.</u> Be careful about jokes in the office. People can be easily offended. Jokes that rely upon racial, gender, religious, or ethnic stereotypes are dangerous ground. Vulgar jokes are out out out.

3. <u>First impressions last.</u> Work on your first impression; make a good one. When you meet someone look him or her in the eye. Shake hands with a firm squeeze, avoiding on the one hand, the bone-crunching grasp and, on the other, the limp, jellyfish touch. Introduce yourself with the name you would like to be called. Address others by the names they prefer; it is not your prerogative to shorten Elizabeth to Liz. As you are taken around a new office greet everyone this way. When you attend meetings, say hello to everyone while looking them in the eye. (There was a saying at the National Security Agency, an organization filled with shy computer geeks, that you could tell the difference between extroverts and introverts. Extroverts would stare at your shoes rather than their own.)

4. <u>What to order in restaurants.</u> When eating with your boss or other seniors or clients, particularly including when you are being interviewed, order something that is easy to eat, preferably something that requires a knife and fork. Avoid the quarter pounder with cheese or the taco. It is embarrassing to have meat juice, ketchup, or salad dressing sliding down your arm and chin or squirting onto your tie or scarf. A hint: A meal that requires a knife and fork allows you to take small bites that can readily be swallowed unchewed when you are asked a question. Once during a law firm luncheon interview, I ordered a club sandwich. I soon noticed that every time I took a bite, the interviewing partner would ask me a question. (I think it was his annoying way of seeing how I dealt with stress.) There was then that awkward moment when I raised my index finger to signal that it would take a minute for me to answer and the long pause while I chewed the bite enough to make swallowing possible.

5. <u>Social gatherings.</u> Your boss is your boss and not your friend. Memorize that. Beware of the office gathering or party. Don't treat these events like frat parties. If you over imbibe, you are likely to do or say things that the next day – if you can even remember them – you will deeply regret. I once saw the wife of a summer intern at a large office retreat that offered alcoholic drinks climb up on a table and remove her top. Need I mention that her husband did not get a permanent job offer?

6. <u>Invitations.</u> When your boss invites you to a lunch or dinner, think of this as a command. If you cannot attend, have a really good reason. (A friend in academia tells of inviting a number of students to dinner. A day or two before the dinner, one of the students called to decline explaining that she had "received a better offer.") A thank you note, although now considered old fashioned, is still a nice way to thank the boss for the invitation.

7. <u>Business trips.</u> When traveling with the boss, (s)he is still your boss. Even if (s)he has a drink or two at dinner, be wary of joining in. Do not take business travel as a party at the government's or your company's expense. When on the road, until you

know your colleagues well, go to bed early and get up early. Don't hang out at the hotel bar; don't try to pick up anyone, colleague or stranger.

8. <u>Don't be the ugly American.</u> In our increasingly inter-connected world, it is very likely that in government, NGO, and private sector jobs you will meet and work with foreign nationals, either in this country or overseas. Avoid being the ugly American. Be sensitive to the fact that cultural, social, and religious norms widely vary. We tend to be extremely informal in this country. That is not true in many parts of the world. When meeting with foreign nationals overseas, keep a low profile. Imitate their etiquette, their dress styles, and their behavior patterns. Particularly avoid edgy dress and behavior. One just doesn't wear a bikini in Saudi Arabia. One shouldn't drop the "F" bomb anywhere. In some cultures excessive drinking is taboo. And, of course, don't hit on any of your foreign colleagues.

9. <u>Beware of the office romance.</u> Ideally you will find your mate in some other venue. But realistically, many relationships begin at the office. So if you must, be careful. However, NEVER have a relationship with your boss! The odds of this working out well approach zero, and the things that can go wrong are legion and predictable. Here is how it usually plays out:

a) After a (usually) brief time, (s)he will dump you or you him or her. That makes work life really rough, and when awkwardness sets in – which is usually very soon after the romance cools – you are likely to be the one who is transferred.

b) While you and the boss will persuade yourselves that your little trysts are invisible to coworkers, they are not. Inevitably, colleagues will find out.

c) Then, no matter how meritorious your work, they will believe that your promotion arose or bonus awarded only or largely because of your personal relationship.

d) Inevitably, your colleagues will report your boss to the IG or senior management claiming office favoritism or hostile work environment. And they are likely to win! I cannot overstate how often this happens in offices. (In one office where I worked, a lawyer would leave for lunch. A few minutes later, a second lawyer with whom he was having an affair would leave the office and walk about 20 feet behind him until they reached the restaurant. This routine was repeated on the way back to the office. They became an office joke.)

If you develop a relationship with someone not your boss, keep it out of the workplace. Try to make sure that you and (s)he work in different offices so that your professional paths rarely cross.

10. <u>Seeking dates.</u> Be careful about asking coworkers out on dates. If you ask and are turned down, think hard about whether to renew the invitation. Sure, you might have been turned down because of some genuine calendar conflict. But if the person declines because (s)he needs to rearrange his/her sock drawer, back off. When one continues with unrequited invitations, they begin to look a lot like unwanted sexual advances.

11. <u>Beware of compliments.</u> Avoid commenting on coworkers' appearance. Innocuous comments like "that's a nice tie" or "I really like that suit" are fine. But cross-gender compliments are minefields. They can over time begin to look like attempts to create intimacy and may not be welcome. "You look really hot today" is not likely to be a welcome comment.

12. <u>Don't steal.</u> This may seem obvious, but do not rip off the government or your company. Some people rationalize stealing office supplies by noting the huge waste that occurs in most offices. After all, who cares if you take paper for your home printer, or pens, or toner? The government and your company care. If you are discovered – even if you are not prosecuted – your reputation is forever shot. And if someone is looking for an excuse to get rid of you, your dishonesty provides a great one. Do not pad your

expenses or charge non-business related expenses on the business credit card, even if you intend to pay them back immediately. Do not attempt to stick your employer with expenses that were really for private use. Make sure you know the rules on what is reimbursable and follow them. For instance, if you have to stay over a weekend on a business trip, are you permitted to keep the rental car? May you charge all your meals over that weekend?

13. <u>Know what counts as work.</u> Be judicious about reporting your time and attendance. Your time "networking" or "tweeting" or feeling the pain in the office gym might not meet the IG's or your company's definition of legitimate work or properly billable hour. I once had an employee who routinely claimed exorbitant amounts of overtime. In due course the IG and I were alerted. After an investigation, he was dismissed. He is a prime example of one who stumbled over quarters to pick up nickels.

14. <u>Be polite.</u> Liberally use "yes sir" and "no ma'am." Sometime in the late Sixties or early Seventies the workplace became less formal. All of a sudden senior partners in law, accounting, and lobbying firms became "Bill" and "Nancy," not Mr. or Ms. Smith. Although less true in the government, informality has made inroads there, as well. Do not let the fact that you have been invited to address your boss by his/her first name mislead you into thinking that you are somehow equals. You are not, not even close. Politeness, as demonstrated by the use of "sir" and "ma'am," really does help even if it seems a bit antiquated. Make it a habit and act politely toward everyone both senior and junior.

15. <u>Avoid arrogance.</u> As you move up the corporate or government ladder, do not throw your weight around. Lower level employees can sabotage you. One of the stupidest and most arrogant comments is: "Do you know who I am?" The answer is usually no, and the rudeness doesn't help your cause.

16. <u>Follow office etiquette.</u> Learn the etiquette of your agency or office. In the Department of Defense and some other government agencies, juniors will close their correspondence with "V/R," which stands for "Very Respectfully." Other agencies observe other

forms denoting respect. In some government and private sector offices, people stand when the boss enters the room. Learn these customs. Mimic them.

17. <u>Do not use your boss's name as a license.</u> Do not wrap your boss's mantle around your shoulders. Even if you are his/her executive assistant or principal colleague, do not bigfoot your way around the office. (As a special assistant to a cabinet officer, I once sent a memo asking in the name of my boss for information on some subject I was curious about. When the answer arrived – addressed to my boss, of course – he circled his name on my request followed by a huge question mark. I never made that mistake again.) You would be surprised by the number of young hotshots who have poisoned the well with the arrogance that they borrowed from their boss's position. People will remember. People will get even.

18. <u>Exhibit a positive attitude.</u> Don't whine; do smile. Whiners and complainers are immediately and forever branded. No one wants to be around them, no matter how brilliant and insightful they may be. And their assignments sooner or later will reflect their negative attitudes. People who readily smile and evince enthusiasm are invited to work on every project.

19. <u>Build up others, including your boss.</u> When you begin your first professional job, the odds are high that you will feel insecure. Everyone else, particularly your boss, will appear to be self-confident and above it all. You will assume that they know better and do not need your support or flattery. Alas, what you will learn over time is that virtually everyone, including your boss, has insecurities. Indeed, bosses are often the most insecure players in the office. (Perhaps they became the boss in the first place because they were trying so hard to prove their worth.) Being attuned to other people's insecurities and helping them feel good about themselves will benefit you.

You can earn a lot of goodwill by building others up. You can do this by flattery, by listening, by loyalty, and by letting them take the credit. If this sounds a lot like sucking up, it is: "Wow, that is a great idea!" "I never thought of that!" "Terrific presentation!" "That question [from the Committee Chair, the client, the boss's boss which the boss was unable to answer] was really unfair!" If you are in a meeting with the boss and he is struggling to find the answer to a question, you can subtly provide the answer on a piece of paper that you slip him/her. Let him/her take the credit for your ideas. If you offer a good idea, the boss may pretend in public that the idea was his/hers; (s)he may never acknowledge your contribution. That is okay. Subconsciously you are building trust and reliance. Years ago in private law practice, I once sent red roses to my (male) boss who had been in a grueling hearing on Capitol Hill. On the card I put "you have earned the red badge of courage." Although he was at first a bit embarrassed that he, a man, had received flowers from a man, he was really quite pleased.

The point here is that all of us are tempted to think only of our own problems and needs. By being sensitive to others' insecurities and finding appropriate ways to support your bosses and colleagues, you will engender positive responses and improve the overall morale and tone of the office. So instead of dwelling on your own problems, look around and see what you can do to boost others. Be clever about it and figure out what each of your colleagues and bosses needs and how to respond to those needs.

20. <u>Exhibit equanimity.</u> Avoid the Jekyll and Hyde syndrome, where some days you are pleasant and smiling and others where you are unpleasant and surly. Colleagues appreciate consistent behavior; it is no fun wondering each day which Mary or Joe will show up. Tame your emotions. Don't flip out or have a temper tantrum in front of others. No one wants to work with volcanic people.

21. <u>Do not evangelize in your office.</u> Avoid hectoring about religious, political, or social matters. No one wants to be handed religious or political tracts. No one wants to be harangued about abortion or the death penalty. Avoid aggressive bumper stickers. Do not close your emails with quasi-religious language: Have a Blessed Day.

22. <u>Do not fundraise.</u> Do not take up collections for causes unrelated to the workplace. Yes, I am sure your little dear is a wonderful Girl Scout or Boy Scout and is cute as a button. But most of us prefer to give to charities of our own choosing, not those of our office colleagues. And never seek donations for partisan or hot-button political causes. It will offend some people and might in some contexts even be against the law.

23. <u>Avoid ethical violations.</u> In most government offices, one receives an ethics lecture early on from the general counsel's office. Pay attention. There is a fair amount of conduct that most of us would think nothing about that in fact violates one government ethics rule or another. For example, in the government you are not allowed to let those with whom you are working in the private sector pay for your lunch. Years ago in private law practice, my colleagues and I held a series of meetings with Department of Justice lawyers, sometimes in our offices, sometimes in theirs. When they visited us, they would not accept even a free can of soda, which the firm provided free to its employees. When we ordered lunch, they insisted on contributing their pro rata shares. In the private sector, talk to your boss about any issues that tweak your conscience. The odds are high that your conscience is on to something.

24. <u>Your reputation matters.</u> Ultimately, the most valuable thing that we possess is our reputations. Guard yours like the jewel it is.

# CHAPTER 4

# E-Stuff

Alert: bits and bytes are forever.

1. <u>Your computer can be an undercover spy.</u> Beware of everything you do on the internet, even at home on your own time. Employers are increasingly using Facebook and Google to investigate prospective employees because such inquiries are cheap. Those digital photos of you – hoisting a glass at a bar or in *flagrante delicto* with your lover – may come back to haunt you. Remember, bits and bytes are forever.

2. <u>Be wary of what you do on your work computer.</u> Try never to use your office IT system for personal stuff. Yeah, of course if a coworker emails you about eating lunch, fine; if your spouse emails you about some household emergency, okay. But personal communications may indeed not be so personal. When you push the delete button, there is no little guy inside your computer shredding your deleted communications. Computer forensic experts can often recreate everything you thought you had deleted.

The federal government and most state governments sticker their phones and computers alerting you that these machines are the government's and not yours. You therefore have no reasonable expectation of privacy under the Fourth Amendment. And in the private sector, there is no question that anything you do on the office computer can be monitored. Your employer owns the computer on your desk or laptop and every piece of data on it. Thus, when you surf the net and pull up some porn or play solitaire your IT folks may be alerted by tracking filters. What seems like an innocent email or search today may some day come back to bite you. Again, bits and bytes are forever. Just ask various government officials about misbegotten computer use.

3. <u>Use professional email addresses.</u> Don't use weird or suggestive email addresses for your private email systems: "drunkeveryweekend@aol.com" does not strike the right professional tone.

4. <u>Don't e-impersonate your boss or anyone else.</u> In many offices secretaries and one or two trusted assistants have the password for the boss's computer. This is so when (s)he is out of town, they are able to get on his/her computer to read and respond to urgent messages, of course with the approval of the boss. Don't ever get on his/her computer unless you have express permission and then only for authorized purposes. I once had an assistant who "spoofed" me, meaning he got onto my computer and signed my name to self-serving emails, in order to obtain bonuses and other benefits. Inevitably his scheme was uncovered, he was fired, and his reputation destroyed.

5. <u>Respond to emails.</u> When you receive an email, reply to it (not reply all) unless it is a mass email. It is frustrating to send an email to someone who does not respond. One doesn't know if there were some kind of electronic problem in the transmission. It takes only a few seconds to reply "thanks" or "got it."

6. <u>Think before you push the send button.</u> Beware of sending harsh or over-heated emails no matter how witty and perceptive they seem. It is likely that through the forward button your email will be shared. Either through innocence or guile your email may go viral and be sent throughout the organization or indeed the world. (Just ask certain disgraced politicians and celebrities.) Eventually the object of your ire will see it. I once had an employee who, in response to a mass emailing inviting people to an agency-sanctioned event, blasted the sender for wasting his time. Instead of pushing the reply button, he pushed the reply all button. As a result his ridiculous, petty diatribe was seen by thousands of his coworkers, including all the senior leadership.

7. <u>Respond to accusatory emails.</u> When you receive an email or other correspondence that falsely accuses you of some sort of failing or bad behavior, always respond. Because bits and bytes are

forever, an unchallenged accusation may become part of a record. If you do not respond, an inference may arise that the accusation was accurate. A response need not be nasty in tone. If you are responding to the boss, the response should be polite. A response need not be lengthy. A one liner may suffice: "your account is inaccurate" or "with all respect, boss, that is not how it happened."

8. Use the reply all button judiciously. The reply all function is a useful technology when you are part of a group that is exchanging information and views on drafts, strategies, and the like. But in most agencies and many private sector offices, seniors are flooded with emails about things they could not care less about simply because someone pushed reply all. The head of an agency once asked me to order a person in my department to stop cc'ing him on emails.

9. The reply all can be useful. Where reply all can be extremely useful is in summarizing the outcomes of meetings. If a meeting reaches a number of conclusions and sets forth a list of assignments, summarize those decisions and assignments in an email to the boss, copied to the team. Conclude the email with something like: "If I have missed something, please let me know."

10. Beware of the heated response. When you are the recipient of a hostile email, ponder your response overnight. The great thing about communications 40 years ago was that the extant technology effectively required a delay in responding. By the time the nasty response had been typed, edited, and finalized, the drafter might conclude that the response was overwrought. Now with the convenience of the reply button, it is easy to send an ill-thought-out, unduly harsh response that one will regret in the morning. I and many of my friends have at one time or another regretted sending a hasty response to an unpleasant email. Draft your response, save it in drafts, and review it the next day. The odds are high that you will delete it.

11. Be temperate in commenting by email. You, along with many other addressees, will frequently be asked to comment by email on draft papers, briefs, letters, or ideas. If your comments

are critical or lengthy, be polite and push the reply button, not the reply all button. The party who is seeking comments will appreciate your consideration in not making public your harsh criticism. By sharing your criticism with other recipients, you may well be viewed as a braggart trying to show how bright you are.

12. <u>To email or not to email: that is the question.</u> Concerning particularly sensitive and contentious issues, ponder whether you really should use email. The advantage of email, of course, is that it provides a record of your advice. The disadvantage is that it provides a record of your advice. Emails in the government are subject to Freedom of Information Act requests, meaning that on contentious issues it is likely that your advice will become public. In both the public and private sectors, emails may be "discovered" during litigation, meaning that they may become evidence in a case. Moreover, emails can be perceived as cowardly cover-your-ass memos: "I told the boss today that he should not go forward with the project because it might be unlawful." Your boss will appreciate an oral communication on potentially embarrassing or sensitive matters. When I held senior government positions, I never used email to discuss sensitive issues. Rather, I exchanged information face to face.

13. <u>Two important questions.</u> About every use of your computer ask yourself two questions: a) would I care if my boss saw this document or read this email? b) Would I be embarrassed if this document or this email appeared in *The Washington Post* or *The New York Times*?

14. <u>Voice mail etiquette.</u> When using voice mail, always immediately provide your name, phone number, and time when you called. Enunciate clearly. Abbreviate your message. It is annoying and frustrating to listen to some long, rambling message only to wait and wait and wait for the crucial information: the caller's name and his/her phone number. If the phone number is unclear, then one has to go through the entire tedious message just to get to it again. It should be obvious, but my experience suggests it is not: do not mumble and race through the phone

number. Your own phone number of course is second nature to you; it is not to others. And provide the number in a recognizable sequence. Not 70-35-55-12-12, but 703 [pause] 555 [pause] 1212. Then repeat the number.

# CHAPTER 5

# Resumes

Creating resumes: Don't make it complicated.

1. <u>Keep it relevant.</u>   There are entire books devoted to resumes. There are lots of companies that will help you write up your resume for a fee. I have received resumes on extremely fancy bond with a number of different type faces. Some even exude a scent. My experience in the public and private sectors suggests that this is a waste of your money. When I review the resumes of applicants I look for a very few items: where they went to school and graduate school, if relevant; what they majored in; what their grades were; what foreign languages they know and what, if any, academic awards or honors they received. In other words, I am interested only in stuff that relates to the job being sought. Years ago when I worked in a law firm, we received a resume from a third-year female law student that, under hobbies, listed modeling and then set out her measurements. This information might have been relevant for some job, but not for a law firm job.

I have never cared and I don't think most prospective employers will care that you babysat the summer before your junior year in high school, that you were chosen as most likely to succeed by your fraternity or sorority, that you teach Sunday school, that you were president of your senior class in high school, or that your hobby is building model airplanes. I have seen all of these on resumes. Of course, if you have a skill or expertise that is relevant to the job, mention it. For example, in the government intel biz that you know foreign languages may well be relevant. Or if you have some sort of computer literacy or programming skill, that would certainly be relevant to any job requiring that knowledge. If you have published something serious, mention it.

2. <u>Keep it brief.</u> Employers receive tons of resumes. You have perhaps half a minute to impress. Most employers look askance at long resumes, for there is often an inverse relationship between the length of a resume and the quality of a candidate. It is the rare candidate who needs more than a page for a resume. I have worked professionally for over 35 years, and my resume is still only one page. If the position for which you are applying requires a detailed description of, for example, your prior positions, skills, or publications, include this information as an attachment. This will allow the prospective employer to focus on the highlights on the first page before getting bogged down in the details.

3. <u>Blemishes.</u> It is difficult to cover up holes or hide blemishes in one's resume. You must decide whether it is worthwhile even to try. For example, I have seen resumes that do not list graduation dates, presumably because the applicants thought they might be viewed as too old. I have seen resumes whose work histories revealed one- or two-year gaps. When employers notice these lacunae, they may feel that applicants are trying to hide something, for example, a period of unemployment or even jail time. Thus, you must decide whether to reveal something that is not creditable or to try to hide it from an employer, gambling that (s)he may not notice the time gap. Be sure to think about it carefully, weighing the options (and odds of being caught!) before choosing how to proceed. It may be appropriate to explain a gap in your resume or an unusual educational sequence in a cover letter. This allows you, without lying, to put it in the best possible light before the prospective employer jumps to the worst conclusion.

# Reach the Author

This book recounts office experiences that friends, colleagues, and I have witnessed. I would love to hear the stories of readers. I can be reached at <u>holdthatjob@gmail.com.</u>

Made in the USA
Charleston, SC
21 September 2014